THE
MIDDLE EAST
IN SEARCH OF
PEACE

Updated Edition

Cathryn J. Long

THE MILLBROOK PRESS
Brookfield, Connecticut

Published by The Millbrook Press
2 Old New Milford Road
Brookfield, CT 06804
© 1996 Blackbirch Graphics, Inc.
First Edition

5 4 3 2 1

Created and produced in association with Blackbirch Graphics.
Series Editor: Tanya Lee Stone

Library of Congress Cataloging-in-Publication Data
Long, Cathryn J.
   The Middle East in search of peace/Cathryn J. Long. — Updated
   ed/
   p.   cm.
   Includes bibliographical references (p.   ) and index.
   ISBN 0-7613-0105-4
   Summary: In covering the 1993 signing of the peace pact between the
P.L.O. and Israel, this book explores the origins of the Arab-Israeli conflict,
previous peace plans, and the implications of the historic recent agreement for
the future.
   1. Jewish-Arab relations—1949—Juvenile literature. 2. Israel-Arab conflicts—
Juvenile literature. I. Title.
DS 119.L66 1996
956.04--DC20   96-21421
                                                    CIP

Contents

Chapter 1

Handshake in Washington

On the morning of September 13, 1993, President
Bill Clinton was up before dawn working on a
welcoming speech. That day, the White House was
going to host the signing of a peace agreement between
the Israeli and Palestinian people. These peoples had been
in conflict over the same lands and rights in the Middle
East for a long time.

But their fight was not simply a local one. Jewish
people all over the world felt that they had a stake in
Israel—a state founded as a homeland for all Jews. And
the Arab countries bordering Israel had become embroiled
in the struggles of the Palestinians. The whole world had
teetered on the brink of disaster more than once, as the
United States and Soviet Union seemed about to join the
battle. Oil price increases connected with the conflict had
also caused economic turmoil in many parts of the world.
For all these reasons, this chance at peace was extremely
important. The eyes of the world were on Washington,
D.C., that September morning.

As the sun rose, White House aides made last minute
preparations for the crowd of 3,000 that would attend the
signing ceremony on the White House lawn. All of the

The world
welcomes a
ray of hope
for peace in
the Mideast

Opposite:
President Clinton looks on as
Israeli Prime Minister Yitzhak
Rabin and Palestine Liberation
Organization Chairman Yasir
Arafat shake hands at the
momentous signing of the
1993 peace agreement.

members of Congress had been invited. So had three former presidents and their secretaries of state. Representatives of foreign governments joined Mideast experts, leaders of American Jewish and Arab groups, and the press. Many reporters had followed the Israeli-Palestinian conflict for decades. One of these reporters remarked that he had long said, "Hair will grow out of the palm of my hand before Israel will allow the Palestinians to hold elections in Gaza and the West Bank." Yet that was just one of the many things the treaty to be signed that day would do.

Two Major Participants

As the sunny morning progressed, the crowd members settled into their seats and the major participants of the event filed up to a platform. The two people who were to formally sign the agreement were Foreign Minister of Israel Shimon Peres, and Mahmoud Abbas, a high-ranking official of the Palestine Liberation Organization (PLO). Standing next to them were U.S. Secretary of State Warren Christopher and Russian Foreign Minister Andrei Kozyrev. They were to sign as witnesses, as their countries co-sponsored official Israeli-Palestinian peace talks. Missing from the podium, but happily present in the audience, was a group of Norwegians who had a key role in the talks in Oslo, Norway, that had helped to bring about the agreement.

At the center of the platform group stood President Clinton, beaming, and on either side of him the two men everyone really wanted to see: Prime Minister Yitzhak Rabin of Israel and PLO Chairman Yasir Arafat. The two had been lifelong enemies. Having them stand together on the same platform was quite an event. People wondered if they would finally look each other in the eye and shake hands. The gesture would be a sign of sincerity, and would offer some proof that this new peace could last.

Shimon Peres signed the 1993 peace agreement as the representative of Israel.

Yitzhak Rabin spent most of his life as a soldier. He fought for the Allies (the United States, Great Britain, Soviet Union, France, and China) in World War II, and then fought the Arabs to help create the state of Israel in 1948. After that, Rabin became an important general in the Israeli army. In 1967, in one of several wars between Israel and Arab countries, he led Israeli forces in capturing areas where many Palestinian refugees had been living since losing their homes in Israel. These areas, the West Bank, Gaza Strip, and Golan Heights, became Israel's "occupied territories." The peace agreement would authorize a limited form of self-rule by the Palestinians in the West Bank and Gaza Strip until a permanent form of rule could be worked out. After 1968, Yitzhak Rabin held three major posts in the Israeli government: ambassador to the United States, minister of defense, and prime minister twice.

Rabin had said that he had many terrible memories of conflict with the Palestinians, from comrades killed in battle to innocent Israeli victims of Palestinian terrorism. Yet from the beginning of his term as prime minister in June 1992, he sought peace with his old enemies. Three days before the 1993 peace agreement signing, Rabin

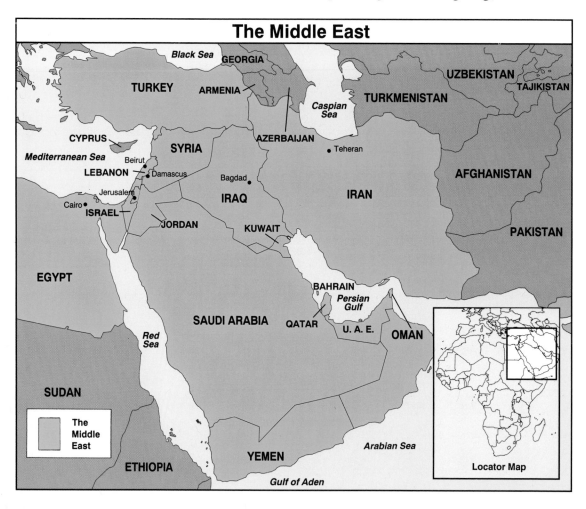

The Middle East

exchanged letters with Arafat, in which each recognized the other's authority, and opened the door for signing the agreement. Explaining his position, Rabin said he was tired of the endless fighting. "Enough of blood and tears," he said. "Enough." Rabin himself later became a victim of the conflict he tried to stop. At a peace rally in 1995, he was assassinated by an Israeli opposed to his policies.

Yasir Arafat had an equally long history of struggle. Like most Palestinians, he lived much of his life in exile. He was born in Jerusalem, and lived as a boy in the Gaza Strip. Educated in Cairo, Egypt, Arafat worked as an engineer in Kuwait. There, in 1956, he founded the Al Fatah organization to fight for the restoration to Palestinians of land captured by Israel. Arafat and Al Fatah joined the PLO in 1968, and he became its chairman the following year. He has held that post ever since.

From its beginning, the PLO claimed to represent all Palestinian Arabs. Arafat helped direct terrorist raids on Israel, and cooperated with Arab nations in their conflicts with Israel. He encouraged the Intifada, or resistance, which arose in the occupied territories in 1987.

For twenty years, Arafat was banned from the United States because he supported terrorist activities. But on September 13, 1993, welcomed in Washington, D.C., he held out his hand to Rabin, his old enemy. As the two grasped hands, the crowd broke into long, roaring applause.

In the early 1990s, Yasir Arafat, chairman of the PLO, stated his desire for peace and democracy in the Middle East.

Main Points of the Peace Agreement

The agreement signed in Washington, D.C., called for peace between the PLO and Israel in exchange for limited self-rule in the West Bank and Gaza Strip. The agreement specifically called for five years of limited self-rule by the Palestinians. During that time, a permanent final agreement would be negotiated. The exchange of control would begin in the Gaza Strip and in Jericho, which is an ancient city located in the West Bank.

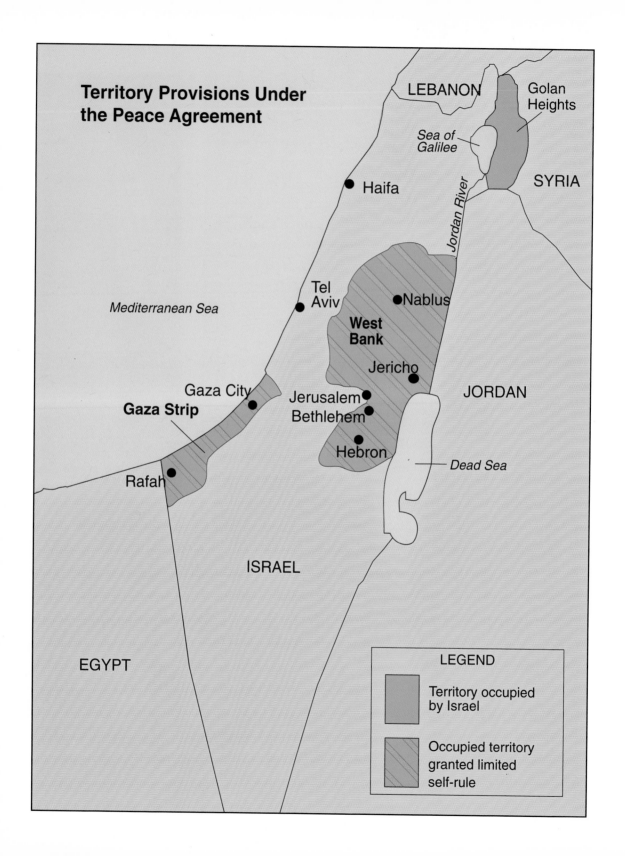

Territory Provisions Under the Peace Agreement

LEBANON

Golan Heights

Sea of Galilee

SYRIA

Haifa

Jordan River

Tel Aviv

Mediterranean Sea

Nablus

West Bank

Jericho

JORDAN

Gaza City

Gaza Strip

Jerusalem

Bethlehem

Hebron

Dead Sea

Rafah

ISRAEL

EGYPT

LEGEND

Territory occupied by Israel

Occupied territory granted limited self-rule

Under the agreement, Palestinians would hold elections within nine months of the signing to create their own governing council. The council would take on the duties of local government. A Palestinian police force would be created. This police force would replace Israeli soldiers. Israelis would only guard borders, some roads, and Israeli settlements within the territories. The agreement, or accord, also called for disputes between Israelis and Palestinians to be settled by a joint committee.

An Israeli soldier guards a post on the Israeli border in the Golan Heights.

Secret Meetings in Oslo

One day in December 1992, an Israeli history professor walked into a London hotel room. He was there for a secret meeting with a PLO representative. The meeting was unofficial—and illegal. Officially, peace talks had been going on for two years between Israel and a Jordanian-Palestinian delegation in Madrid, Spain, and Washington, D.C. Legally, Israelis were prohibited from talking to PLO members because of its opposition to Israel.

The secret meeting took place because things were changing. Official Israeli negotiators had realized that the real power behind the Palestinians at the talks was the PLO itself. And the newly elected government headed by Yitzhak Rabin had decided to try new ways to achieve peace. The London meeting was not the only secret, "back-channel" effort to reach an agreement. But it was the one that eventually succeeded.

In the London hotel room, the two men exchanged ideas and agreed they would like to talk more about broad issues. Each gained an OK from higher officials. The question remained: How and where to meet again? They needed secrecy and safety. Those would be hard to achieve in the Middle East, or even in a major world city. Luckily, both Yair Hirschfield, the professor, and Ahmed Khoury, the PLO official, knew members of the Norwegian Institute for Applied Social Science. The Institute was at work in the West Bank and Gaza Strip, where its experts were studying living conditions. The head of the Institute, when contacted, was quick to offer help. He arranged with the Norwegian government to host discussions in and around Oslo.

Beginning in January 1993, fourteen sessions of a few days each were arranged over eight months. The delegates were flown in separately to avoid attracting attention. Norwegian police took them to meeting places. There, the delegates were supported by well-informed Norwegians. Two couples helped especially with the talks. One was Foreign Minister Johan Holst and his wife, Marianne Heiberg, leader of the Norwegian study of the occupied territories. The second pair was Terje Larsen, head of the Institute, and his wife, Mona Juul, a Norwegian foreign ministry official.

The Norwegians helped build an atmosphere of trust between the Israeli and Palestinian. After long sessions, the delegates walked together in the woods, ate together, and watched TV news and videos. They even played on the floor with the foreign minister's four-year-old son, Edvard. An Israeli noted, "To say the atmosphere was friendly is an understatement."

As the secret talks continued, the two sides found more common ground. By May, they had drafted a peace agreement. At that time the Israeli legislature had overturned the law against talking to the PLO. Two Israeli officials were sent out to help with revisions to the draft. By August 20, Israel and the PLO had initialed the agreement. When U.S. officials in Washington, D.C., were informed, they were surprised—and pleased. Although they had known that the meetings had taken place, they did not expect such dramatic results. President Clinton was quick to express U.S. support by hosting the signing, and special invitations were sent to the Norwegians.

This farmhouse, near Oslo, Norway, was the location of secret meetings between Israeli and PLO officials in 1993.

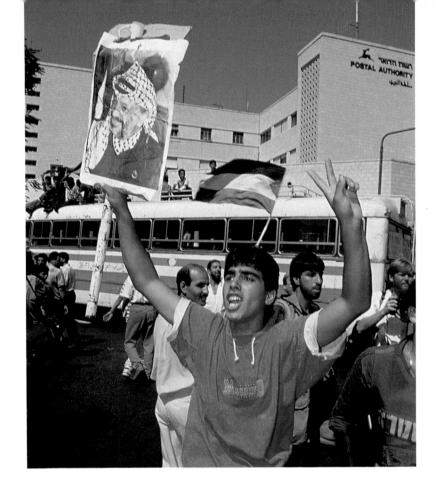

Palestinians parade in joyful celebration after the signing of the peace accord in September 1993.

Israelis and Palestinians would carry out joint economic development in the Gaza Strip and West Bank. Their efforts would be strengthened by aid from around the world. This economic provision was especially important because of the extreme poverty of people in the territories.

Many matters remained unsettled or vague under the agreement. What would happen to Jerusalem, which both Israelis and Palestinians claim as their capital? How many refugee Palestinians from other areas would be let into the territories? What would be the fate of Jewish settlements in the territories? There were no immediate answers. The agreement claimed to be a "declaration of principles," and not a list of particular solutions.

But beyond these was a larger, more fundamental question: Could a lasting peace survive after such a long history of conflict?

14

Chapter 2

A Long History of Conflict

T he 1993 accord called for an end to a conflict that had a long history behind it. The conflict had roots that preceded Israel's creation in 1948, and has continued with renewed force ever since. In the years since that time, Israelis and Palestinians have fought in five wars and have mistreated, threatened, and launched terrorist attacks on each other in between those wars.

At the same time, some Palestinian Arabs have lived peacefully as citizens in Israel. Many Palestinians and Israelis have friendly relationships. And, as President Clinton pointed out at the signing of the agreement, Jews and Palestinian Arabs both claim to be part of the ancient family of the Biblical figure Abraham. These positive facts may add to the promise of real peace between Palestinians and Israelis at last.

Palestine and Israel

The state of Israel did not exist before World War II. The region that Israelis and Palestinians both think of as home is a strip of land along the Mediterranean north of Egypt once called "Palestine." The name comes from one of the

Tension between Arabs and Jews runs deep and has been hard to overcome

Opposite:
Clouds of smoke rise above a Jerusalem building set on fire. This occurred during Israeli-Arab conflicts that followed a U.N. partition of Palestine into separate Jewish and Palestinian states in 1947.

many tribes that once lived there, the Philistines. The Palestinians of today are descendants of some of the earliest inhabitants of the region, who intermarried with people who arrived later.

The Israeli Jews of today also have ancestors from Palestine's earliest days: the Hebrew tribes. By 1000 B.C., the Hebrews had formed a kingdom in Palestine, called Israel. For a time, the kingdom was divided into two parts called Israel and Judah. The term "Jew" originally meant a Hebrew who was from Judah. Later, the word Jew was used to refer to all Hebrews.

Through much of its history, however, Palestine was ruled by foreign powers. In the first century A.D., the Roman rulers of Palestine feared a Jewish revolt. They forced most Jews to leave the land. Jews spread out around the world in a diaspora, which means a great scattering. Some, however, remained in Palestine.

By the fourth century A.D., Christianity was firmly established in Palestine. In the 600s, the Arabs invaded Palestine and introduced a religious faith called Islam. With it they brought the Arabic language and Islamic culture. Today, most Palestinians are Muslims (followers of Islam) and speak Arabic. However, some Palestinians did remain Christian.

The Jews, meanwhile, settled in many other countries. Intermarriage and economic success made some feel at home wherever they were, as generations continued. However, many Jews were treated unfairly because of their religion. In the fifteenth century, Jews were driven from Spain, where they had lived for hundreds of years, when King Ferdinand and Queen Isabella decided all of Spain should be Catholic. Four hundred years later in Russia, Jews were forced to live in separate districts, or villages. The Russian czars encouraged peasants to attack the Jews in terrible raids called pogroms. At the beginning of the twentieth century, many Russian and other European Jews emigrated to the United States. Today, the United States

Opposite:
Muslims at prayer in an Islamic temple, or mosque. Most Palestinians follow the traditions of the Islamic culture.

has the largest Jewish population of any country in the world, about twice as many as live in Israel.

In the 1890s, some European Jews started a movement to create a nation of their own. They called the movement Zionism. The name came from Mt. Zion, a hill in Jerusalem where a great Israeli king, Solomon, built a temple. Zion later came to mean all of the Jewish homeland in Palestine. Between 1900 and 1914, 40,000 Jews moved to Palestine. They settled alongside Palestinian Arabs and minority groups of Christians and Middle Eastern Jews. Most Palestinians at this time were farmers who grew olives, fruit, grain, and sesame using traditional methods. Some Palestinians were Bedouins (a tribe of nomadic Arabs) who moved from place to place with their flocks of goats or sheep. The land was dry, and the soil was poor. Few Palestinians were wealthy.

From the beginning, the newly arrived Zionists did not get along with the Palestinians. The people living in the area resented foreigners buying up land. Many European Jews had more money and education than did the Palestinians. They seemed to be taking over the area. But the Jews felt that they too had a right to their homeland.

At that time, the area of Palestine had been part of the Turkish Ottoman empire for over 400 years. After the Turks were defeated in World War I, the League of Nations gave Britain the right, or mandate, to rule until the people of the region could govern independently. The part of Palestine that was east of the Jordan River was renamed Transjordan and British authorities established an Arab leader, Sherif Hussein there. (After World War II, Hussein became king and his country, now called Jordan, gained full independence.)

The part of Palestine that was west of the Jordan River was ruled by the British, who inherited the conflict between Palestinians and Jews. This was a problem because, during World War I, Palestinian Arabs had fought with the British to throw off their Turkish rulers. In return,

British leaders had promised them eventual independence. Then, the British also promised the Jews the right to a homeland in Palestine. This promise was made official in the Balfour Declaration, a statement made by British foreign secretary Arthur Balfour in 1917. Later, the promise became part of the legal mandate for Palestine issued by the League of Nations.

Many more Jewish people poured into Palestine in the years just before and just after World War II. During the war, Jews faced the worst assault in history by German Nazis. Over six million Jews were murdered as part of the Nazi Holocaust. Survivors were desperate to find a refuge and Palestine seemed like the logical place to go.

By 1947, about 600,000 Jews were living in Palestine, though Arabs outnumbered them by more than two to one. Conflict between the groups focused on their British rulers. Frustrated, the British gave up the territory to the United Nations and a U.N. plan divided Palestine into a Jewish area and three Palestinian areas. These areas were to become one Jewish state and one Palestinian state.

Warfare began between Jews and Palestinians even before the British left Palestine. On May 14, 1948, the day before the official British departure, Israel declared itself a nation. On May 15, five neighboring Arab states quickly declared war on Israel and rushed to the aid of the Palestinians. By the end of the year, Israel controlled an area a little larger than the land that was marked for it in the United Nations plan. Under a cease-fire arranged in January 1949, Jordan, Egypt, and Syria controlled other parts of western Palestine. Half a million Palestinian Arabs had fled their homes in Israeli territory.

As a result of the war, the state of Palestine envisioned by the United Nations had disappeared. Some Palestinians spread out in a kind of diaspora. Many, however, were too poor to travel anywhere. The United Nations set up camps for these Palestinians outside Israel's borders. In the camps, resentment toward Israel grew.

This synagogue, the largest one that existed in Berlin, Germany, was set ablaze by the Nazis during an anti-Jewish demonstration in November 1938.

THE 1947 U.N. PARTITION

Conflicts Continue

In addition to locations in Egypt's Sinai Peninsula, the refugee camps and Palestinian villages outside of Israel became centers from which raiders called *fedayeen* (literally, freedom fighters) attacked across the border into Israel. In reply, the Israeli army attacked the villages and camps. Destruction of property and deaths on both sides led to increased hatred and fear. Israel asked for aid and arms from the West (the United States and western Europe). Egypt, which helped fund and arm the *fedayeen*, was also looking for aid. Egypt's leader, Gamal Abdel Nasser, tried to play off the West against the East (the Soviet Union and its Communist allies). If he did not get aid from one, he said, he would seek it from the other.

With tensions high between East and West, the United States and its allies decided not to give Nasser aid for a big economic development project, the Aswan Dam. An angry Nasser seized the Middle East's most important waterway, the Suez Canal connecting the Mediterranean and the Red seas, from its French and British owners in 1956. From then on, he said, it would be run by and for Egypt. Next, he closed the canal to Israeli shipping. The Israelis then made a secret agreement with France and

A Palestinian walks away from a *fedayeen* base after an Israeli air raid hit this Lebanese town.

Britain to try to overthrow Nasser. Israel attacked Egypt via the Sinai Peninsula. The Israeli army did destroy some *fedayeen* command posts, but the attack on Egypt soon failed in the face of world opinion. In the end, Egypt kept the canal. Israel managed without it by shipping via a new port, Eliat, built at Israel's southernmost point. The Suez War proved to be the first of many conflicts in which Arab opposition to Israel, triggered by the Palestinians' grievance, flared into violence and threatened world peace.

In the years after the Suez crisis, the Arab countries were upset by revolutions and civil war. However, Saudi Arabia, Kuwait, and some other Arab countries enjoyed a windfall of new wealth from oil. In 1961, oil-rich countries formed the Organization of Petroleum Exporting Countries (OPEC). They hoped to use this new wealth to gain global respect—and to finance the Arab struggle against Israel. In 1964, Arab heads of state, meeting in Egypt, established the Palestine Liberation Organization. It was to act as an umbrella organization for Palestinian groups living in various Arab countries. Its purpose was to promote the struggle against Israel.

In 1966 and 1967, raids across Israel's border increased. Nasser and other Arab leaders openly threatened Israel. They even set a formal date for invasion in 1970. Finally, in 1967, Nasser ordered U.N. patrols out of the Sinai Peninsula and stopped shipping into Eliat by blockading Israeli ports. The Israelis then decided to fight.

The result was the Six-Day War of 1967. Israel gained a great advantage by striking first. On the morning of June 5, Israeli fighters managed to obliterate the air strength of Syria, Jordan, Iraq, and Egypt with their bombing efforts.

The Israelis were not only interested in preventing attacks. They also wanted to create safety zones around Israeli borders. In well-planned attacks, Israel took the Sinai Peninsula and the Gaza Strip from Egypt, the West Bank and East Jerusalem from Jordan, and the Golan Heights from Syria. A cease-fire was arranged within six days, but a shocked U.N. passed a resolution calling on Israel to withdraw. The resolution also called for recognition of Israel by the Arabs. However, neither side would budge.

Nasser died in 1970, but his successor, Anwar el-Sadat, planned a new war on Israel. With Syria, Egypt attacked in 1973 on Yom Kippur, a day when Jews pray and fast. The Yom Kippur War ended within three weeks, with little territorial change. During the war, Arab members of OPEC decided to use the "oil weapon" to promote their cause. They raised oil prices, reduced production, and set an embargo in which they refused to sell oil to the United States and Holland (both of which strongly backed Israel).

In June 1967, Israeli troops passed freely through the Mandelbaum gate, which once separated Jordanian and Israeli Jerusalem.

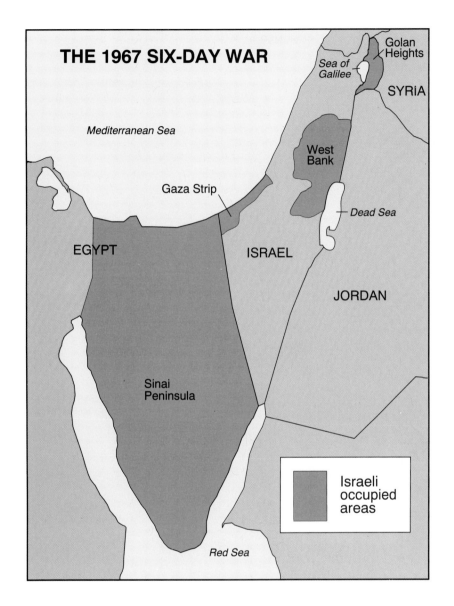

THE 1967 SIX-DAY WAR

Golan Heights

Sea of Galilee

SYRIA

Mediterranean Sea

West Bank

Gaza Strip

Dead Sea

EGYPT

ISRAEL

JORDAN

Sinai Peninsula

Israeli occupied areas

Red Sea

Oil would become easier to get, they said, only if Arab demands were met. The oil crisis continued after the fighting stopped. The global economic upset it caused continued into the 1990s.

Meanwhile, many Palestinians felt that only renewed terrorist activities would draw world attention to their cause. Palestinian groups, including the PLO, set bombs, hijacked airplanes, and took hostages. Jordan became a

During the 1973 oil crisis, Americans had to wait in long lines to buy gasoline at increased prices.

headquarters for PLO troops. Jordan's King Hussein (grandson of Sherif Hussein) did not want to be seen as a sponsor of terrorism. He also felt the PLO was a threat to his authority in Jordan. In 1970, he attacked the PLO with his own army. The PLO troops then moved to Lebanon, where civil war had made that government weak. Terrorism directed against Israel and its allies continued.

In 1977, and again in 1982, Israel invaded Lebanon to attack PLO forces. The Lebanon war that began in 1982 was particularly brutal. Israel's army besieged the capital,

Beirut, for ten weeks. Finally, an international force supervised the evacuation of PLO forces. They were dispersed to nine different Arab countries. A new PLO headquarters was established in Tunis, Tunisia. Then, Israeli forces quickly occupied Beirut. While in Beirut, they allowed Lebanese militia, who were hostile to Muslims, to enter Palestinian refugee camps. The Lebanese militia murdered over a thousand helpless men, women, and

The Palestine Liberation Organization

The Palestine Liberation Organization (PLO) was accepted by Israel as the legitimate representative of the Palestinian people in the 1993 peace agreement. Before and since the signing of the accord, though, the PLO's right to that title has been challenged. What exactly is the PLO, and what is its relation to the Palestinians of the occupied territories?

The PLO became what it is today in 1968. The reason can be traced to events in the village of Karameh, Jordan, in that year. In Karameh, a pocket of Palestinians, members of Al Fatah, were still fighting Israel after the end of the 1967 war. The Israeli army warned that it would attack the village, and told people to leave. Either Yasir Arafat or another Al Fatah commander (stories vary) made a speech urging the *fedayeen* to take a stand against the Israelis. Less than 300 fighters held off 1,500 Israeli troops all morning. Boys strapped explosives to their bodies and threw themselves in front of Israeli tanks, blowing up themselves along with the tanks. In the end, most of the Palestinian fighters were killed. Yasir Arafat, one of the survivors, became a Palestinian hero overnight. New recruits flocked to join Al Fatah.

Arafat, the hero of Karameh, attracted the attention of Egyptian President Nasser. Nasser felt the PLO, which represented Palestinians in Arab countries since 1964, was not close enough to the anti-Israel struggle. He urged the PLO to

reorganize so Al Fatah could merge with it. The PLO became a confederation of independent Palestinian organizations. Representatives of these groups meet and vote as part of the Palestine National Council (PNC). As president, elected by the PNC, Yasir Arafat holds most of the power in the organization.

However, Arafat's power is far from absolute because the groups in the PLO are free to act independently. Often, they oppose or ignore what Arafat wants. In order to move the PLO as a whole, Arafat must always create a consensus—gain the agreement of all the member organizations. However, consensus is not always easy to achieve. By the beginning of 1994, half of the members of the Executive Committee had resigned. They claimed Arafat was not listening to their points of view.

As a result of the peace agreement, the PLO has begun to change into something more like a political party. Instead of organizing attacks or ordering secret activities, it is sponsoring certain candidates and policies. In the first Palestinian elections, held in January of 1996, Yasir Arafat was elected head of the new Palestinian government. His office has legal limits. He is responsible to the voters. The same is true of the PLO candidates who won a majority of seats on the Palestinian Council. The old organization of *fedayeen* is becoming part of a democracy.

Hostile Lebanese militia approach women in a Palestinian refugee camp in Beirut, Lebanon.

children. People all around the world, including many Israelis, were horrified. Israel finally withdrew its army in 1985, though the Lebanese civil war did not actually end until 1991. The conflict between Israelis and the Palestinian people, however, remained unabated.

The Intifada

The conflict reached a major crisis point in December 1987, when Palestinians living in the occupied territories began a revolt known as the Intifada.

The uprising was, in part, a reaction to the living conditions of the Palestinians in the territories. Palestinians in the occupied territories have lived partly in refugee camps, and partly in towns and villages. Camps were first set up with tents in 1949. Since then, cement block houses have replaced the tents, but most facilities like water and sewers have been generally inadequate. Most roads and paths are unpaved, turning to dust in the summer and mud in the rainy season. Overcrowding and poverty have added to the misery. Very few Palestinians have had jobs. Some work has been available in Israel, although it is usually the less-skilled and lowest-paying jobs that are open to Palestinians. Over the years, Palestinians have commuted to Israel on long bus rides, or waited at village street corners for Israeli employers to pick up truckfuls of workers for a day's hard labor.

A house in the Jewish settlement of Efrat, in the West Bank, is built by Palestinian laborers. Many Palestinians resented having to work for Israeli employers.

Seeds of Peace

A fifteen-year-old boy was talking about getting along at summer camp. "In the beginning it wasn't easy. It wasn't like we said, 'Hi, we're friends.'"

Most kids who have been to camp would recognize the feeling. But few have been to a camp like the one this boy attended. Seeds of Peace Camp was founded in 1993, just before the signing of the peace agreement, to bring Israeli and Arab youth together. Campers here often begin by thinking they are bunking with the enemy.

Seeds of Peace operates for three weeks every summer in Maine, far from the strife of the Middle East. It was founded by American John Wallach, former foreign editor for Hearst Newspapers. Wallach wanted to encourage peace by allowing people who had been taught hate to get to know one another as human beings. Teenagers, Wallach thought, were still young enough to learn new ways. The 130 campers come from Israel and the occupied territories, plus neighboring Jordan and Egypt.

Campers find that even ordinary routines are complicated because of cultural differences. Boys and girls must swim separately, for instance, because Muslim rules require it. Israeli campers celebrate the Sabbath weekly with special food and prayers. And Arab campers stop to pray at certain times each day—even if they happen to be in the middle of a soccer game.

However, it is the shared activities and the talk that make a difference. After long days of shared sports, campers meet in the evening for discussions. Trained counselors are there to help smooth the way. The teenagers talk about the ideas of one another that they grew up with. They talk about why it's so hard to be friends. Over time, barriers begin to fall. Many Israeli and Arab children who live only a few miles apart in Jerusalem and the West Bank have become friends in the past three years.

An Israeli and an Arab boy take a break together after playing baseball.

In the unhappy setting of the camps and villages, anti-Israeli feeling has always had a home. The Intifada, however, was a new kind of battle. It involved civilian resistance to Israeli rule by every means possible. Beginning in 1987, many Palestinians refused to pay taxes to Israel, or went on strike to protest Israeli rule. Palestinians harassed or attacked Israeli soldiers. They refused to give information to Israeli authorities. They flaunted the flag of the United

Palestinian boys look on as one child holding a United Arab Emirates flag throws stones at Israeli soldiers who have just passed by.

Arab Emirates, which became a badge of rebellion. Palestinian men, women, and children all took part in the Intifada—especially children. Many young Palestinians felt they had no hope for a good education, a job, or a happy future in the grim conditions of the occupied territories. They threw stones, set fires, and shouted insults at the enemy in defiance.

Israeli responded to the Intifada with arrests, beatings, and collective punishment. In some cases, Israeli authorities blew up the houses of suspects whose families refused to give information. Sometimes whole camps were placed on curfew, meaning in this instance that no people or goods (including sometimes water and electricity) could go in or out. Deaths and disappearances became common. Some kidnappings and killings were even carried out by Palestinians angry at other Palestinians who were thought to be aiding the Israelis.

The Intifada greatly increased suffering, hostility, and fear between Israelis and Palestinians. At the same time, it helped make the situation so intolerable that both sides were forced to seek an accord.

Chapter 3

Building the Accord

The signing of the accord in Washington, D.C., was both a beginning and an end. It represented the first step on a long and, at times, treacherous road toward peace in the Middle East. No one is completely confident that Palestinians and Israelis will ever reach their destination of total reconciliation.

The accord was also the final step along another road that was no less long or troubled. Nations worldwide have been involved in the bitter dispute between these enemies for years. Some, particularly the United States, have worked to end the conflict. In this sense, the accord represented the culmination of the efforts and influence of many countries.

Obstacles to Peace

For those nations seeking peace, the obstacles have been many. "This land is really ours." This statement represents a conviction, held by Israelis and Palestinians alike, that has been the major obstacle to any lasting peace. This

> The difficulties of creating peace are felt by all those involved in this struggle

Opposite:
Baghdad, Iraq's capital, is bombarded during the 1991 Persian Gulf War. The war proved to be a turning point in Arab-Israeli relations as it forced many Arab nations to align themselves with Israeli allies for the first time.

conviction has roots that are ethnic, cultural, religious, and even legal. Each side claims God gave the land to its ancestors to hold for its people forever. Each claims to be the side that has acted fairly. Palestinians say the Israelis unfairly removed them from lands their families had held for generations. Israelis say they were mistreated by the world, generation by generation, and that the world owes them one place to call home. Both point to promises made by the British government while it ruled Palestine. Those promises could not be reconciled.

A related obstacle to peace has been the mutual hatred and fear that has been caused by events since the founding of Israel. In this relatively small area, there is no individual who has not been personally touched by the conflict. Everyone has more than one relative, friend, or neighbor who has been killed, wounded, or badly treated by the other side. Living with constant conflict has led to tension and distrust. One Israeli has said, "Now the Palestinians are trying to take from us the feeling of being home and

Young Palestinians demonstrate their support for the Palestine Liberation Organization in 1992.

we won't let them. They cannot take from me my basic right to feel at home here." According to a West Bank student, "I think our generation of Palestinians has reached a point psychologically where we want any means of getting back at the Jews. You just get the feeling that the Jews want to aggravate us." Throughout most of the history of Israel, Palestinians have refused to acknowledge Israel's existence, and Israelis have refused to negotiate with the PLO.

Another kind of obstacle to peace has to do with the nature of the land and the people who live on it. Historically, Palestine has not had an adequate supply of natural resources, especially water. Neither side has wanted to share these precious resources with the other. At the same time, the Palestinian population has grown at a rapid rate. While the Israeli birth rate has not been as high, Israel has been accepting Jewish refugees for years. In the early 1990s, Jews from the former Soviet Union came by the hundreds of thousands. These population increases have caused problems such as housing shortages for all the people of the area. Perhaps the sorest point has been employment; many believe that as a result of immigration, jobs in Israel once held by Palestinian Arabs have been given to Jewish newcomers. Without massive aid from outside, the tendency to fight for scarce jobs and resources would only increase with time. All of these unresolved conflicts have stood in the way of any real peace in the Middle East.

Peace and the World

People around the world learned what the value of Mideast peace is firsthand when gasoline drastically shot up in price in 1973. The Arab oil embargo forced everyone to see what a stake the world has in the Mideast. Even before that time other countries made efforts to end the Arab-Israeli conflict.

The Water War

In the Middle East, there is one resource that is more precious for the people than oil—water. Without it, crops cannot grow, industry cannot function, and people cannot survive. With the growing population, water is becoming even more scarce in a land that is naturally dry. As a result, Israel, the Palestinians, and neighboring countries have been arguing over water rights. "If there's no agreement on water," said one Jordanian expert, "there'll be no peace settlement."

The major sources of water for Israel and its neighbors are the Jordan river system and aquifers. An aquifer is a layer of porous rock that stores water from winter rains. Deep aquifers contain water that cannot be replaced because rain does not filter down far enough.

The Israelis have taken full advantage of the water they can reach. They pump water from sources of the upper Jordan located in the Golan Heights. The Sea of Galilee, into which the upper Jordan flows, acts as Israel's chief reservoir. A national pipeline system takes water from the sea south to most of Israel.

Jordan is very short of water. In recent times, Jordanians could not even use Jordan River water because the Israelis were pumping salty spring water down it from the Sea of Galilee. Jordan does tap a major tributary of the Jordan, the Yarmuk River. Yet that river has less water because it is dammed upstream by Syria. In between is rising the new and thirsty voice of the Palestinians.

Water for the West Bank today comes from wells that tap an aquifer. Israel has saved and regulated the supply of water by limiting the number and depth of the wells. People in the West Bank in 1993 used only 30,360 gallons (115,000 liters) of water per person, per year. By contrast, Israelis use 100,320 gallons (380,000 liters) per person, per year. The Israeli water services modern agriculture and industry, plus a standard of living that includes, for most people, a sink, a dishwasher, a washing machine, a shower, and a toilet. As the West Bank strives for the same, limits on water use will have to change and new water will have to come from somewhere. In the Gaza Strip, the situation is also desperate. Aquifer water there is nearly gone.

Some progress has been made in solving the water problem. The Israel-Jordan peace agreement of 1994 included adjustments of water rights that pleased Jordan. Part Two of the Israeli-Palestinian peace agreement, reached in 1995, promised a larger share of water to West Bank dwellers via new or improved water sources. Finally, though, the last word on water will have to come from two agreements that still lie in the uncertain future. Syria's peace with Israel will have to include a water settlement; water was a major source of conflict between the countries before the 1967 war. Water has also been named as a major issue to be settled in the permanent agreement that the Israelis and Palestinians hope to reach by 1999. With luck, that settlement will encourage use of modern technology such as desalting plants that may increase the water supply for all.

Annual Water Consumption Per Person

	Israel	Jordan	Gaza Strip	West Bank
gallons	100,320	37,000	34,320	30,360
liters	(380,000)	(140,000)	(130,000)	(115,000)

Source: The Israeli Consulate.

Many hoped the United Nations would bring peace to the Middle East. It has played a role, though not a major one, in the region since 1948. Sometimes United Nations resolutions helped set an ideal. U.N. Resolution 242, which passed after the 1967 war, called on Israel to withdraw from lands it had taken in the war. At the same time, it asked Arab states to recognize Israel and agree to peace. Resolution 242 expressed the "land for peace" idea that lies behind Israel's 1979 peace treaty with Egypt, and behind the 1993 peace agreement.

The United Nations also served Israelis and Palestinians in other ways, such as monitoring cease-fires and hearing complaints regarding border violations. Perhaps its most valuable long-term service has been its practical help for Palestinians living in refugee camps.

Why didn't the United Nations become a stronger force for peace? One reason is that members of the body did not always agree on the goals for the Middle East. In the past, the East-West conflict sometimes interfered. During the 1960s, many new developing nations became voting members of the United Nations. They tended to support the Palestinians, whom they thought of as a poor and oppressed people like themselves. Many resolutions condemning Israel were passed with their votes. And, even when most members agreed on a resolution, backing it up depended entirely on the willingness of members to provide military power. For this reason, the United Nations was said to have few "teeth."

A U.S. Concern

The Arab-Israeli conflict has been a major concern of the United States since the year Israel was founded. One reason is that Israel is a close ally. The United States government sends large amounts of aid to Israel every year. Along with support for Israel, the United States has had two other major goals in the Middle East. One was

President Eisenhower speaks to the United Nations General Assembly in August 1958 about his proposal for stabilizing conflict in the Middle East.

to contain communism and keep global peace. The other was to keep oil flowing to the world from the invaluable Middle East oil fields. Conflict between Israelis and Arabs worked against all of these goals. As a result, the United States tried to stop conflict, especially when it flared into open warfare. For example, President Dwight Eisenhower led the move in the United Nations to achieve a cease-fire in the 1956 war—even though old U.S. allies, Britain and France, had helped start the war. President Lyndon B. Johnson held a special summit meeting with Soviet leader Andrei Kosygin to make sure the 1967 war did not spread. President Richard Nixon joined his Soviet counterpart to help end the 1973 war. Nixon also sent Secretary of State

Henry Kissinger on several "shuttle diplomacy" missions to try to arrange peace among Arab leaders and Israel after the 1973 war. By 1975, the missions resulted in three disengagement accords. Each accord returned some Israeli-conquered land to an Arab country in return for peace promises.

The United States also helped sponsor the greatest breakthrough for peace before 1993: The 1979 peace treaty between Israel and Egypt. Egyptian President Anwar el-Sadat started the move toward the treaty in 1977. In 1978, when discussions stalled, U.S. President Jimmy Carter invited Sadat and Israeli Prime Minister Menachem Begin to the United States. The men met at Camp David, the presidential retreat near Washington,

President Jimmy Carter with Egyptian President Anwar Sadat (seated left) and Israeli Prime Minister Menachem Begin (seated right) at the ceremony for the official Camp David accords in March 1979.

Sadat's Visit to Jerusalem

On November 19, 1977, the unthinkable happened in Israel. A plane touched down at Jerusalem's airport carrying one of Israel's greatest enemies— on a mission of peace. Anwar el-Sadat, president of Egypt, had planned the Yom Kippur War against Israel only three years before. With his Arab allies, he had sworn not to recognize or negotiate with Israel. Yet on this day, he had decided to change that. Bravely he had come to seek peace talks, and Prime Minister Menachem Begin was his host.

Why did Sadat choose to talk to the Israelis? It seems he had decided Israel was on the map to stay. After losing several wars with Israel, Sadat felt that some new tactic was needed. He decided to seize the moment after the 1973 war when, despite the fact that they had not won, Egyptians felt proud of their effort. Sadat then felt he could negotiate with Israel from a position of honor. Peace would mean Egypt could stop spending so much money on war with Israel. It could also mean that aid and better trade with the United States and other western countries could enrich Egypt. Sadat promoted world peace when it was not popular among his own people.

"You want to live with us in this part of the world," Sadat said, in a speech to Israel's legislature. "In sincerity I tell you that we welcome you among us with all security and safety." He asked in return that Israel give back the lands it had taken in the 1967 war. He also pointed out "the core of the problem" between his country and Israel—the need for a Palestinian homeland.

There is no doubt that Sadat astonished the Israelis and persuaded them to seek peace, too, at the risk of looking bad to the world. Sadat's visit led to negotiations that ended in the Camp David accords. One of the accords became a formal peace treaty between Egypt and Israel, signed in 1979. The other accord laid plans for a Palestinian homeland. It was neglected until the 1993 agreement gave it life at last.

The 1993 agreement, however, came too late for Sadat. Many Egyptians and other Arabs grew angry when nothing was done to give the Palestinians a home. The Arab League expelled Egypt for making peace with Israel, and wealthy Arab countries cut off aid to Egypt. Despite U.S. aid, the Egyptian economy drooped. In an atmosphere of public discontent, Muslim fundamentalists opposed to the government assassinated Sadat on October 6, 1981. His successor, Hosni Mubarak, has managed to follow in Sadat's efforts at peace. He has actively aided both Israelis and Palestinians in working out the specifics of the 1993 and 1995 peace agreements.

Anwar Sadat (right) speaks privately with Menachem Begin (left).

D.C. Together, they reached the "Camp David accords."
One accord became an official peace treaty between Israel
and Egypt, signed in 1979. According to the treaty, Israel
returned the Sinai Peninsula to Egypt (though it kept the
neighboring Gaza Strip). In return, Egypt became the
first and, to date, only Arab country to recognize Israel
and agree to a full peace. Prime Minister Begin and
President Sadat were awarded the Nobel Peace Prize for
that achievement.

The United States backed up the peace treaty with
promises of massive, equal aid for both Israel and Egypt.
To this date, those nations receive more U.S. foreign aid
than any other country.

A second part of the Camp David accords was called "A
Framework for Peace in the Middle East." For the first
time, it called for independence for the West Bank and
Gaza Strip under Palestinian rule. The accord was never
put into effect because the PLO refused to consider it at
the time. Its goal then was still to take all of ancient
Palestine for their people. However, the framework set
down some of the basic ideas later included in the 1993
peace agreement.

A New Context for Peace

In 1991, two events occurred that made a big difference
in the search for Mideast peace. One was the Persian Gulf
War. That war began when Iraq invaded Kuwait, apparently hoping to take both the tiny country's oil wealth and
its seaports. In response, Arab countries joined in a sur-
prising alliance with the United States and other Western
powers to push Iraq back. Thanks largely to United States
firepower, that goal was quickly gained. New bonds
joined the Arab world to Israel's old friends.

Meanwhile the Israelis had not joined in the Gulf War,
at the request of the United States. Even when Iraqi
shells hit some targets in Israel, there was no shooting

back. If Israel had fought Iraq, the conflict might have turned into another Arab-Israeli war, with Arab countries shifting over to Iraq's side. Iraq certainly wanted that to happen. Despite Iraq's verbal and shell attacks on Israel, no Arab country gave its official support. The PLO and Jordan only offered verbal support. These words turned out to be costly. Wealthy Arab oil states cut down aid to Jordan and to the PLO. When Yasir Arafat saw his Arab support slipping, peace with Israel may have looked more attractive.

For their part, the Israelis worried about the new partnership between their greatest ally, the United States, and the Arab countries. Their concern probably made them more willing to negotiate with the Palestinians to keep American good will.

A second major event of 1991 for Arab-Israeli relations, and for all the world, was the final formal breakup of the Soviet Union into a group of republics. For several years, the Soviet Union had been shedding its old communist identity. The end of the Union meant that the old East-West rivalry was gone. The United States no longer had to defend Israel against communist power in the Middle East. Also, the United States had emerged as the single most powerful nation in the world. Its wishes could not be very easily countered or ignored—especially by people who needed large-scale economic aid.

The U.S. government seized the moment immediately after the Gulf War to campaign once again for an Arab-Israeli peace. President George Bush sponsored new talks along with Russia, the strongest nation of the former Soviet Union. The co-sponsors pressured the Israelis and Palestinians, as well as neighboring Jordan, Lebanon, and Syria to come to the peace table at Madrid, Spain. Talks began there November 3, 1991, and moved to Washington, D.C., in the next year.

At the official peace talks, the conservative Israeli government headed by Yitzhak Shamir, who had replaced

Menachem Begin as prime minister in 1983, was slow to agree to anything. The Likud political party had been elected in Israel to protect and keep Israel as it was. It did not favor change and even stepped up Israeli settlements in the West Bank. Finally, President Bush decided to hold off loan guarantees for the housing of Israel's flood of Soviet immigrants. This move added to Shamir's problems at home. There, economic recession and the immigrant tidal wave were making life difficult. In an election in 1992, the Israeli conservatives lost power and the Labor party was voted in. The United States welcomed this new leadership, and it was under the Labor party that the 1993 peace breakthrough was achieved.

Yitzhak Rabin campaigning for the Labor party during the 1992 Israeli elections. The Labor party took power after the Likud party was voted out.

A city worker in Jerusalem scrapes election posters off a wall following the defeat of the Likud political party in 1992. Yitzhak Shamir is pictured on the Likud party posters at top.

There was an essential difference between the Oslo talks that led to the 1993 peace agreement and many of the other Mideast peace talks of the past. This was the fact that Israelis talked to PLO representatives alone, face-to-face. Since the 1948 war, most Israelis and others around the world had thought of the Palestinians as really Jordanians, Syrians, Egyptians—people belonging only to the country that they were living in. That is why one Israeli prime minister, Golda Meir, said of the Palestinians, "They do not exist."

Palestinians began to regain their identity when Israel took over the West Bank and Golan Heights at the end of the 1967 war. They found themselves under one government—that of their enemy. The PLO expanded and, through organization and social work, became a kind of shadow government recognized by most Palestinians in the territories. Then, in 1987, the Intifada set a seal on Palestinian identity. Some observers have said that without that civil uprising, the Palestinian people might have completely lost their identity and become simply less privileged Israelis.

Official peace negotiations, meanwhile, largely ignored the Palestinians' claim to be a people who should speak for themselves. The Camp David accords were created by Israel and Egypt—even the part that had to do with the future of the Palestinians. The Madrid negotiations did not include the Palestinians as full negotiators. Instead, a Palestinian delegation was attached to the one that was sent from Jordan.

Matters did not change until 1992, when Israelis elected the Labor party government under Prime Minister Rabin. This new government decided that peace could be met with the PLO itself. That was why the September 1993 handshake between the Israeli prime minister and the PLO chairman that took place in Washington, D.C., meant so much. At last, each side was speaking to the other in person.

Chapter 4

Step by Step Toward Peace

Within eight months of the signing of the 1993 peace agreement in Washington, D.C., forty Palestinian Muslim worshippers were gunned down by a Jewish settler in the West Bank town of Hebron. In the same period of time, the Gaza Strip and Jericho were peacefully transferred from Israeli to Palestinian control. The first of these two events shows the kind of fearful violence that has occurred as the peace accord takes effect. The second event is evidence that despite opposition, delay, and violence, the accord is being made a reality—step by step.

Opposition from Both Sides

Opinion polls have shown that most Israelis and Palestinians favor the peace agreement and the changes that it is bringing. Yet opposition to all or part of the agreement has been fierce on both sides. Often this opposition has delayed the timetable of the accord, and has even threatened to bring it to a halt.

In the past, many Palestinians felt that Israel had no right to exist. Some continue to say that the land of Israel should be entirely "returned" to the Palestinians. This

Unresolved issues make a lasting peace in the Mideast uncertain

Opposite:
More than 100,000 Israelis crowded Tel Aviv's municipal square on November 4, 1995, to show support for peace-making policies.

On February 27, 1996, a Jerusalem bus was blown up by terrorists connected to Hamas.

concept was written into the charter of the PLO, even though Yasir Arafat has been willing to accept a smaller Palestine for many years. The PLO's Palestine National Council assembled in February 1996 to remove the old wording from their charter.

Even if the PLO admits Israel's right to exist, however, other Palestinians organizations do not. Two anti-Israel groups in the territories, Hamas and Islamic Jihad, emphasize Arab unity under the Muslim faith. Both have also favored violent acts against Israel and against the peace process. Some of the worst violent incidents in the Middle East since 1993 have been carried out by these groups. In 1995, for instance, two members of Islamic Jihad set off bombs in Israel that killed 19 Israelis—and the bombers themselves. In February and March, 1996, suicide bombers linked to Hamas killed people in Jerusalem busses and at a Tel Aviv shopping mall. Spokesmen for the bombers said they were done in revenge for killings of Palestinians by Israelis.

The cycle of revenge and resentment is hard to break. When Palestinians harm Israelis, the Israeli government usually reacts by closing the borders between Israel and the occupied territories. Israeli authorities imprison Palestinians who may be suspects or have information. They press the Palestinian Authority, in charge of areas policed by Palestinians, to do the same. Army patrols increase. These measures keep Palestinians from their jobs in Israel and make innocent Palestinians more resentful of Israel than ever.

A major tactic of the Israeli government is to hold Yasir Arafat and his new Palestinian government responsible for all acts of terrorism against Israel. Arafat's task is extremely difficult. A terrorist may be working only with a small, secret group—almost impossible to find or stop. And, even when a violent incident is sponsored or accepted by a Palestinian organization, Arafat does not always want to condemn everything that organization does. Already, Arafat has been accused of being a tool of the Israeli government. If he loses the trust of many Palestinians, his position as leader could become meaningless and the peace process could fail.

Among Israelis, opposition to the peace process comes from two main sources: politically conservative Israelis and the Jewish settlers living in the occupied territories.

The conservative Likud party in Israel officially opposes the peace agreement. Even though the pro-peace Labor party has been in power since 1992, the accord would be undone if Likud were to win a majority in an election.

As a group, the 140,000 Jewish settlers in the West Bank and Gaza Strip are very conservative. Most of them are strongly religious Jews who view the territories as part of Eretz Israel, the Israel described in the Bible. Even before the peace agreement was signed, the settlers were demonstrating against it. Their clashes with Palestinian neighbors have led to an increasing death toll.

Because the Jewish settlements dot all of the Palestinian territories, they are potential flashpoints of further conflict. How to deal with them is one of the most important matters to be determined as part of the peace process.

A New Phase of the Peace Agreement

For months following the signing of the peace agreement in 1993, the PLO and Israeli government talked and talked. Their aim was to nail down just how territory was to be transferred from Israeli to Palestinian authority. Delays and violence made some people say it would never happen. Then, finally, between May 13 and 18, 1994, the Israeli army withdrew from the area of Jericho and from almost all of the Gaza Strip. Palestinians gathered in crowds to celebrate the event, which they saw as liberation. This step made all parties feel the agreement was going to work. Further assurance came from Yasir Arafat. He moved into a house in Gaza City with his wife, ending a long period of wandering exile.

The 1994 Nobel Peace Prize went to Yitzhak Rabin, Shimon Peres, and Yasir Arafat for reaching the 1993 peace agreement. However, the leaders still had more work to do in arranging specific actions to carry out the

In recognition of the 1993 peace agreement, the Nobel Peace Prize was shared by Rabin, Peres, and Arafat.

principles stated in 1993. Finally they agreed to a Part Two of the peace agreement. Yitzhak Rabin and Yasir Arafat returned to Washington, D.C., to sign the new agreement on September 28, 1995.

Part Two of the peace agreement carried out the principles stated in the first accord by naming specific places and times for Israeli withdrawal from Palestinian areas. Within six months, the Israeli army was to withdraw from the West Bank's seven largest cities: Nablus, Jenin, Tulkarm, Qalqilya, Ramallah, Bethlehem, and part of Hebron. It was then to withdraw from 450 smaller Palestinian towns and villages. The Israeli army would redeploy, which means move to military bases in the Palestinian countryside or move to protect Jewish settlements and certain roads. The first redeployment would remove most Palestinian people from Israeli military rule; but it would leave 70 percent of Palestinian land in Israeli control. Further redeployments, to take place every six months, would leave all the West Bank and Gaza Strip under Palestinian control except for areas to be named as part of the final permanent arrangement. That arrangement was to be made by 1999.

As the army redeployed, the Part Two peace agreement called for election of an 88-member Palestinian Council and a head of government. Palestinians greeted the agreement as a step toward becoming an independent nation with its own democratic system. On the subject of Palestinian independence, Prime Minister Yitzhak Rabin said, "Now I am opposed; I stress the word 'now.' In the future we will seek all sorts of solutions."

Just over a month after signing the second part of the peace agreement, Prime Minister Rabin went to speak at a peace rally in Tel Aviv. A hundred thousand Israelis had come to support him and the peace process. Rabin gave his speech, sang a "Song of Peace" with the crowd, then tucked the words of the song into his pocket. As he moved to get into his car, a man shot him dead. The

Hamas

Hamas is a word made up of the Arabic initials for an organization called the Islamic Resistance Movement. In Arabic, the word *hamas* also means zeal, or religious passion. Members of Hamas are full of emotionally charged zeal to regain Palestine. Their official goals are to destroy Israel and establish an Islamic state of Palestine that would be part of a greater Arab union.

Hamas was created in the Palestinian refugee camps of the Gaza Strip two months after the Intifada began, in 1988. Like the PLO, Hamas worked to support Palestinians in daily life and to support the Intifada. It gained money from the Islamic fundamentalist government of Iran, and from private Arab donors. The money was used to run clinics and schools and to back chamber of commerce candidates. Today, Israeli experts estimate that 95 percent of Hamas money is spent for such peaceful purposes.

However, Hamas has another side. Violence and self-sacrifice are considered acceptable means to its goals. Young Palestinians have been drawn to the religious and political appeal of Hamas. It gives them an outlet for their rage. Wearing black head covers, Hamas members have been able to demonstrate and attack enemies without being recognized. Some of the most extreme Hamas members have volunteered as suicide bombers. They tape explosives to their bodies under their clothes. Once in a target area, they set the explosives, killing themselves and the people around them.

A rash of suicide bombings killed scores of people in Israeli cities in February and March, 1996. Some of these bombings were claimed by Hamas members as revenge for the death of the Hamas master bomb maker, Yahya Ayyash. Ayyash was assassinated, probably by Israeli secret service agents. Some Hamas leaders, however, distanced themselves from the bombings. They were trying to pursue a chance at gaining strength as a political party under the new peace agreement.

In March 1996, Israeli Prime Minister Shimon Peres declared "war" on Hamas because of the suicide bombings. The split or disagreement within Hamas was apparently forgotten in the Israelis' rush to do something about the bombings. In a replay of life before the 1993 accord, Israeli soldiers descended on Palestinian villages and camps, closing them off, rounding up people for questioning, and sealing families of the dead Palestinian bombers out of their homes. Terrorism and the reaction it brings make the road to peace rockier than ever.

assassin, 25-year-old Yigal Amir, was a Jewish law student opposed to the peace agreement.

Israelis were especially shocked that Rabin's murderer was one of them—instead of an Arab enemy. Although several other people were connected to Amir's crime, the killing was not the result of a large conspiracy. Still, Amir acted upon angry views that had been voiced by many people in Israel. The assassination gave frightening proof that division and violence inside Israel could threaten as much as an outside enemy.

Shimon Peres was soon named by his party as the new Prime Minister. He did not hesitate in following the

The assassination of Yitzhak Rabin was devastating for Israel—and for the world. President Clinton was among several leaders who spoke at Rabin's funeral.

timetable set by the Part Two agreement. Within ten days of Rabin's assassination, Israelis began to withdraw from Jenin, the first West Bank city on the list. The army redeployed from other parts of the West Bank with relatively few problems. Palestinian police took over peacekeeping duties.

On January 20, 1996, Palestinians gathered at polling places in the West Bank and Gaza Strip for the first regional election most of them had ever participated in. On one ballot, voters elected members of the Palestinian Council. On a second ballot, they elected a chairman, or president.

Before the election, Hamas, Islamic Jihad, and other Palestinian groups opposed to the agreement had declared they would not take part. However, they promised not to disrupt the voting. Yasir Arafat was elected head, and many members of his Fatah organization were elected as Council members. Some Council members were elected without Arafat's official support.

An elderly Palestinian woman holds her election card as she waits to cast her vote in the first Palestinian elections.

The most important thing about the election was that 70 to 85 percent of voters turned out in nearly every district. By voting, the Palestinians showed they support the peace process. The new government in the territories can now claim to have the solid backing of the people.

Several international observers were present at the Palestinian election, including former British prime minister Margaret Thatcher and former president Jimmy Carter. They agreed that for the most part, the elections were fair and free. A large number of Palestinian women, as well as men, came to the polls. One of them said, "After years of occupation, it's good to feel free again and that you can choose your own future. Really, it's a great feeling."

Jordan and Syria Stretch Toward Peace

As Israelis and Palestinians took the first steps of the accord and faced their own problems, two neighbors prepared for full peace. Jordan was ready to sign a peace agreement with Israel by October 1994. Syria began negotiations that lasted into 1996.

Jordan governed the West Bank and East Jerusalem from the time of Israel's founding until the 1967 War. When Israel took over the West Bank in 1967, Jordan, as fellow Arabs, sympathized with the Palestinians living there. Yet Jordan's relations with the Palestinians have not been entirely easy. In 1970, Jordan's King Hussein chased PLO troops from his country because they threatened his rule. By the early 1990s, Palestinian immigrants and refugees in Jordan far outnumbered Jordanian natives. Yet the top positions in Jordan's government remained reserved for natives only. That was one sign that King Hussein was worried about being overwhelmed by Palestinian wants and needs. The king also faced another threat—that of Jordanian fundamentalist Muslims. Their challenge to the government pushed the king back toward friendly relations with the PLO. King Hussein used to assume that, in the end, he would keep control over all the Palestinians. Since the accord, he has had to treat them more as partners.

Jordanians and Israelis signed an official peace treaty on October 26, 1994, ending a state of war that had existed on paper between the countries for 46 years. The treaty gave Israel's guarantee that the Palestinians would not try to expand their border into Jordan. Certain lands and water rights were returned to Jordan. Jordan also gained from Israel the right to oversee certain Muslim holy sites in Jerusalem. Perhaps most important, the treaty allowed Jordan to receive economic aid, which was greatly needed, from the West.

A joyous celebration marked the signing of the peace accord between Israel and Jordan in October 1994.

Many Palestinians were angry over the treaty between Israel and Jordan because they felt it left them out. In particular, they objected to Jordanians being in charge of religious sites in Jerusalem—the city they considered to be their own Palestinian capital.

Most of these problems were ironed out in an accord for "mutual cooperation," which Jordan and the Palestinians reached in early 1995. In this pact, Jordan promised to transfer the religious sites to Palestinian hands if and when they gained the right to govern the eastern part of Jerusalem. The pact also encouraged trade and cultural ties. However, one matter often mentioned in earlier talks

Shimon Peres

Shimon Peres became prime minister of Israel 18 days after the assassination of Yitzhak Rabin. Yet Peres was no newcomer to political office. One of the last of the living founders of Israel, he had worked for his country all of his life.

Shimon Persky was born in 1923 in an area then part of Poland. When he was 11 years old, his family moved to Palestine. Persky took the name "Peres," which in Hebrew means the family of birds to which the eagle belongs. He spent his teenage years on a kibbutz, an Israeli cooperative farm. With other young activists, he hoped for an independent Israel.

In 1946, at a Zionist conference in Switzerland, young Peres met a major figure in the founding of Israel: David Ben-Gurion. Peres became an aide to Ben-Gurion and worked for him in establishing the new Israeli government after 1948. In 1952, Ben-Gurion gave Peres the highest civil service job in Israel: director-general of the Defense Ministry. In that post, Peres bought arms, especially from the French. The arms helped make the Israeli army one of the world's most technologically advanced.

As an elected member of the knesset, Israel's parliament, Peres attempted to follow Golda Meir as the next prime minister in 1974. He lost the election to a fellow Labor party leader, the general and political newcomer Yitzhak Rabin. Rabin and Peres were to be as often rivals as friends over many years.

Rabin was forced to resign in 1977 because it was revealed that he held an illegal American bank account. The conservative Likud party took over. Then, in 1984 Peres helped put together a joint Labor-Likud government. Under terms of the two-party agreement, Peres became prime minister for two years. After that, Likud leader Yitzhak Shamir took over. Finally, in 1992, Rabin won the office back and made Peres his foreign minister. In that position, Peres personally sponsored the special effort that led to the 1993 peace agreement. Peres also wrote a book, *The New Middle East*. In it he tells of his vision for a peaceful middle east, with its own common market to encourage trade, and with technology and knowledge to improve life for all.

In the prime minister's seat, Peres has hardly had time to work on his vision. His first task has been to end the violence and keep the peace process alive.

was dropped: the idea of Jordan and Palestine joining as a double country, or confederation.

Like Jordan, Syria had officially been at war with Israel for many years. Syria was eager to exchange peace for the land it lost to Israel during the 1967 War: the Golan Heights. However, since 1967 some 13,000 Jewish settlers have come to live in the Golan. Even more important, fresh water there supplies Israeli towns and farms. These matters, plus the question of Israel's security, have kept Syria and Israel from reaching a quick agreement. If and when they do, peace will probably also come to Lebanon, where Syria controls the government. Southern Lebanon, next to the Golan Heights, is still patrolled by Israeli soldiers and is still home to Palestinian refugee camps.

A Permanent Peace

The 1993 peace accord called for negotiations on a permanent solution to the Palestinian problem within five years. Part Two of the accord repeated this time frame, even though other parts of the agreement have been so much delayed. Talks on a permanent peace were scheduled to begin in May 1996 and end by May 1999.

The questions to be settled permanently are major ones. The future of Jewish settlers is high on the list. It seems unlikely they will be forced to disband and return to Israel. However, the cost to Israel of protecting and supporting them all may prove too great. It is a cost that must be measured both in money and in death, injury, and anguish. While settlers remain in the territories, the Israeli army must remain also. The location and size of military outposts must be negotiated.

A second major question is what the future of Jerusalem will be. Both Israelis and Palestinians claim it for their capital. At the moment, though, Israel has the upper hand. At the end of the 1967 War, Israel did not simply occupy East Jerusalem, as it did the rest of the West Bank.

Hanan Ashrawi

In traditional Arab culture, few women have a chance to lead. Religious rules and social customs keep most women to the sphere of home and family. Few women hold outside jobs, and still fewer enter politics. Among Palestinians, as among Arabs in other parts of the middle east, this pattern is slowly changing. One woman who has broken the pattern completely is Hanan Ashrawi. Professor of English and Dean of Arts at Birzeit University in the West Bank, she has had a hand in Palestinian politics since the 1967 War. In 1996, she was easily elected to the first Palestinian Council.

Hanan Ashrawi has been an important force in Palestinian politics for 30 years.

Hanan Ashrawi is one of five daughters of a Palestinian Christian doctor. She says her parents never dampened her or her sisters' hopes and dreams. She was sent to college in Beirut, Lebanon. From there she went on to graduate school in the United States. As a literature professor, she could have had an easy life in exile from her homeland. But she chose to return to Ramallah in the West Bank to teach.

During the Intifada, Ashrawi helped organize several demonstrations and defend students against Israeli army attacks. She met, often secretly, with Palestinians and Israelis who were eager to end the constant strife. Her contacts increased until she became well known as a Palestinian spokesperson.

In 1991, the U.S. State Department asked Ashrawi and other Palestinians not directly attached to the PLO to take part in talks in Madrid on a possible peace with Israel. The talks were the beginning of a process that ended with the breakthrough in Oslo and the 1993 accord. Ashrawi did not approve of everything in the accord. She thought the West Bank and Gaza Strip areas were too separated. She wanted guarantees of Palestinians' rights, especially in Jerusalem. However, she was happy to accept the improvements the agreement brought to Palestinian life. It allowed her to establish the Palestinian Independent Commission on Citizens' Rights. As Commissioner General, and as a Palestinian Council member, Hanan Ashrawi can continue the struggle for her people and for a just peace.

Instead, it officially annexed the area and united all Jerusalem, making it Israel's capital. The United Nations planned international status for Jerusalem back in 1948 because it is a holy site for Christians, Muslims, and Jews around the world. Various major events in the history of each religion occurred there. The question of who rules and controls entry is therefore of worldwide importance.

In the 1996 Palestinian elections, Palestinians in East Jerusalem were allowed to vote—but only if they cast their votes in suburban districts. The city government was claiming that East Jerusalem was not a Palestinian area. In the final settlement, Palestinians will argue that their history and their population on the ground in East Jerusalem gives them the right at least to that part of the city.

Other unsettled questions include water, borders, and refugees. Somehow, the scarce water in this arid region will have to be divided. Water is vital not just for drinking and farming, but for building modern factories and cities.

The issue of borders for the Palestinians is more complex than it might seem. How will borders between Israel and the territories be controlled, and by whom? How can borders be named in a Palestine dotted with Jewish settlements? How is the 45-mile gap between the Gaza Strip and the West Bank to be handled? These are a few of the questions that must be answered.

Since 1993, Israel has allowed the return of hundreds of Palestinian prisoners and refugees to the West Bank and Gaza Strip. While more wish to return, the issue promises to be less problematic than most others.

Economic development is not on the list of issues to be resolved as part of the final settlement, but no matter is more important. Other nations, especially the United States, have promised aid to the struggling Palestinians. If those promises are not kept, the atmosphere of misery that led to violence and extremism could fully return.

Yasir Arafat and the PLO have claimed all along to want full nationhood for Palestine. In the long run, sovereignty may be a possibility. No nation or people can thrive, though, without peace. The agreements of 1993 and 1995 have given Israel and the Palestinians a chance at that. Shimon Peres of Israel and Yasir Arafat of the Palestinians seem to realize there is no way to continue apart from the peace process. As Prime Minister Peres said after one bus bombing, "We will cope with the pain and suffering, and we will continue with the only way we have, to which there is no alternative."

Chronology

1896	*The Jewish State,* a book by Theodore Herzl, sets the first aims for the Zionist movement. European Jews immigrate to Palestine beginning in 1904.
1917	The British promise the Jews the official right to a homeland in Palestine with the Balfour Declaration.
1947	A United Nations plan divides Palestine into one Jewish state and three Palestinian states.
May 14, 1948	State of Israel is proclaimed. A 7 1/2 month war begins against Palestinians and their allies, which Israel wins, gaining some territory. Arab states lay claim to the rest of old Palestine.
1949	Palestinian refugee camps are established in the occupied territories.
July 26, 1956	Egypt seizes the Suez canal from a French-British company. Israel invades Egypt but withdraws in face of world opinion.
1961	Oil-rich countries form the Organization of Petroleum Exporting Countries (OPEC).
June 2, 1964	The Palestine Liberation Organization is formed by Arab countries.
June 5, 1967	The Six-Day War begins. Israel defeats Egypt, Syria, and Jordan, seizing the Golan Heights, Sinai Peninsula, Gaza Strip, West Bank, and East Jerusalem. U.N. Resolution 242 later calls for Israeli withdrawal from lands in exchange for peace.
1969	Yasir Arafat is elected chairman of a reorganized PLO. Under his leadership, terrorism directed against Israel increases.
October 6, 1973	The Yom Kippur war begins. Egypt and Syria attack Israel. Cease-fire, October 24. Arab oil producers raise prices and cut production to hurt Israel and its allies.
November 19, 1977	Egyptian President Anwar Sadat visits Jerusalem to encourage peace.
September 17, 1978	Camp David accords signed in Washington, D.C., between Israel and Egypt result in a 1979 peace treaty. Israel agrees to return the Sinai to Egypt.
June 6, 1982	Israel invades Lebanon to defeat the PLO there.

December 9, 1987   Palestinians in the Gaza Strip and West Bank begin the Intifada, a continuing uprising against Israeli occupation.

January 1991   The Gulf War begins, in which Arab states join the United States and Western allies to defend Kuwait against Iraq. Palestinians favor Iraq because it threatens Israel. Iraq is defeated in six weeks.

November 3, 1991   Middle East peace talks begin in Madrid, sponsored by the United States and Russia. Israel negotiates with Syria, Lebanon, and a joint Jordanian-Palestinian delegation.

June 1992   Yitzhak Rabin's Labor party wins against the former conservative government in Israeli elections. Rabin actively seeks an accord with Palestinians.

January 1993   Secret meetings take place in Oslo, Norway, between Israeli and Palestinian delegates to begin drafting the peace accord.

September 13, 1993   An agreement is signed between Israel and the PLO granting limited self-rule to the occupied territories.

February 25, 1994   A Jewish gunman opens fire at a mosque at the Cave of Patriarchs, killing at least forty Muslims.

May 13–18, 1994   Israeli troops withdraw from the Gaza Strip and from Jericho as a result of the 1993 peace agreement.

October 26, 1994   Jordan and Israel sign a peace treaty, officially ending 46 years of war and mistrust.

January 26, 1995   Jordan and the PLO sign an accord for mutual cooperation.

September 28, 1995   Part Two of the Israeli-Palestinian peace agreement signed in Washington, D.C.

November 4, 1995   Israeli Prime Minister Yitzhak Rabin is assassinated by Yigal Amir, a Jewish law student opposed to the peace agreements.

November 13, 1995   Israeli troops withdraw from the West Bank town of Jenin, beginning major pullbacks agreed to in the Part Two peace accord.

January 20, 1996   Palestinians elect their own national council and president (Yasir Arafat) in a show of support for the peace process.

March 1996   Four terrorist attacks within nine days in Israel take 62 lives, including those of the suicide bombers.

For Further Reading

Abodaher, David J. *Youth in the Middle East: Voices of Despair*. New York: Franklin Watts, 1990.

Bratman, Fred. *War in the Persian Gulf.* Brookfield, CT: The Millbrook Press, 1991.

Dudley, William. *The Middle East: Opposing Viewpoints*. San Diego, CA: Greenhaven, 1992.

Ganeri, Anita. *I Remember Palestine*. Chatham, NJ: Raintree Steck-Vaughn, 1994.

Morrison, Ian. *Middle East*. Chatham, NJ: Raintree Steck-Vaughn, 1991.

Mozeson, I.E. and Stavsky, Lois. *Jerusalem Mosaic: Voices from the Holy City*. New York: Simon and Schuster, 1994.

Reische, Diana. *Arafat and the Palestine Liberation Organization*. New York: Franklin Watts, 1991.

Steins, Richard. *The Mideast After the Gulf War*. Brookfield, CT: The Millbrook Press, 1992.

Zanger, Walter. *Jerusalem*. Woodbridge, CT: Blackbirch Press, 1991.

Index

Acknowledgments and photo credits

Cover: Nati Harnik/AP/Wide World Photos; pp. 4, 12, 14, 20, 22, 38: AP/Wide World Photos; pp. 7, 13, 31: Esaias Baitel/Gamma-Liaison; p. 9: ©B. Markel/Gamma-Liaison; pp. 11, 58: ©Ricki Rosen/SABA; pp. 17, 28: Chip Hires/Gamma-Liaison; p. 24: UPI/Bettman; p. 26: Gamma-Liaison; pp. 29, 34, 39, 44: Wide World Photos, Inc.; p. 30: Ron Sachs/Seeds of Peace; p. 32: L. Van Der Stockt/Gamma-Liaison; p. 40: Sahm Doherty/Gamma-Liaison; p. 43: Baitel/Hires/Gamma-Liaison; p. 46: Nati Harnik/AP/Wide World Photos; p. 48: ©Waizmann/Action Press/SABA; p. 50: ©Norsk Press Service/Gamma-Liaison; p. 53: Andy Hernandez/Gamma-Liaison; p. 54: Laurent Rebours/AP/Wide World Photos; p. 55: Walker/Gamma-Liaison. Art and maps by Blackbirch Graphics, Inc.